Connemara :
Seaboard of the Horses

Societies of Connemara Pony-breeders

		Secretary
Eire	Connemara Pony Breeders' Society	Mr J. Killeen, 4 Nun's Island, Galway
England	English Connemara Pony Society	Mrs L. Barthorp, The Quinta, Bentley, Farnham, Surrey
Holland	Ver. Nederlands Connemara-Pony-Stamboek	Koniginnegracht 43, The Hague
Sweden	"Svenske Connemaraselskapet"	Fru Karin Johansson, Brantshamarstuteri, 741 00 Knivsta
U.S.A.	American Connemara Pony Society	Alvin M. Mavis, Rochester, Illinois, 62563
Denmark	Danish Pony Breeders Association	K. A. Hartmann, Egtoftewej, 2950 Vedbäk
	Main Association	Dr Merrild, The Hospital, 5970 Aerösköbing
Germany	No society. Interested persons contact K. H. Koellichen	Ponystdelhof, Ziegelei 4, 8191 Gelting, Upper Bavaria

All these bodies were represented at the first International Conference of Connemara Pony Breeders, held at Galway on August 20th–22nd, 1970, under the chairmanship of Lord Killanin and the patronage of the Irish Minister for Agriculture.

Connemara:
Seaboard of the Horses

by

Ursula Bruns

Translated by Anthony Dent

GEORGE G. HARRAP & CO. LTD
London   Toronto   Wellington   Sydney

Originally published in German under the title
"Connemara: Pferdeland am Meer"
© *Albert Mueller* 1969

First published in Great Britain 1971
by GEORGE G. HARRAP & CO. LTD
182–184 High Holborn, London WCIV 7AX

English translation © *George G. Harrap & Co. Ltd* 1971

ISBN 0 245 50622 5

Made and printed in Great Britain by
William Clowes and Sons, Limited
London, Beccles and Colchester

Contents

Note

The bracketed numbers in the text and in the legends under the illustrations refer to the Galway Stud Book.

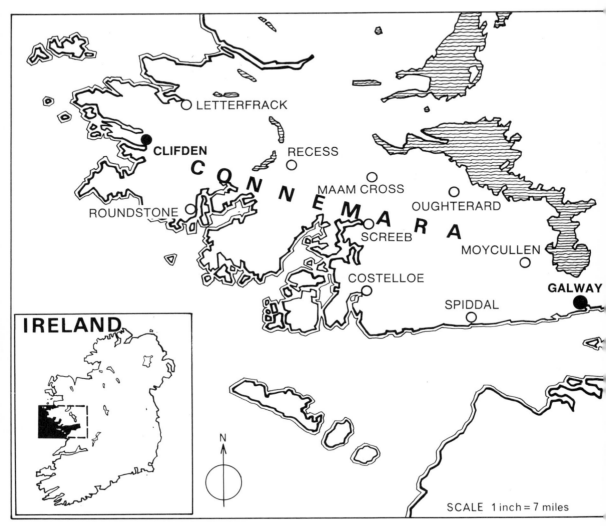

LETTERFRACK

CLIFDEN

RECESS

C O N N E M A R A

MAAM CROSS

OUGHTERARD

ROUNDSTONE

SCREEB

MOYCULLEN

COSTELLOE

GALWAY

SPIDDAL

IRELAND

N

SCALE 1 inch = 7 miles

Reproduced by courtesy of the Irish Tourist Board

> There came a great foaming wave, shooting shorewards,
> Advancing like a warhorse, proud and high-crested
> In the glory of his strength, as it thundered over the surface.
> At the back of this breaker now appeared a lordly rider
> Mounted on a milk-white steed . . . and it leaping behind the billow,
> Skimming the surf, and arcs of foam
> Glinted in the sunlight of morning,
> Spurting with every stride.
> The foamy wave seethed up to the nape of the horse's neck,
> And higher, till only his fiery nostrils showed . . .

The art of the Galway *shanachie* (story-teller) blends the image of the horse and the wave, of the sea-foam and the mane, into such a unity as hardly another poet in the world has contrived.

Iceland excepted, Ireland is the most westerly country in Europe, and Connemara is the western part of Galway, in the West of Ireland. A bulwark against the Atlantic, exposed to all its winter storms, to hurricanes that fling rollers hundreds of feet high against its grooved, fissured cliffs. Countless islets, inlets, bays, and reefs are pounded by perpetual surf, while the wind whips up white tops on the lakes inland, so that the spume drifts away from them like trailing hair. The same wind blows the manes of shaggy ponies high like spray, and makes their tails flutter like a squall of rain across the hillside. What wonder then that horses and wind and sea were seen as one in song and story of the Gaels, perpetuated for ages in the imagination of the hearers? It is only in remote Connemara that boys and girls still hear the poems from the lips of the reciter who is himself a poet, telling his tale by the light of the turf embers, ever improvising anew on themes that were old 'when Homer was a boy'. While without the sea-wind moans softly among the cliffs, he tells how, in the heroic age of the Gaels, 'a shaggy old pony' bore the rider to distant fabulous lands, and helped him out of desperate straits. For here in the thin-soiled land between the rock and the sea it is not by any means always the handsome horse that is the hero of popular story and song. Often the adventurous young prince, setting out on his quest, picks from the well-filled stables of his royal sire 'a little old yellow mare' that will stand him in good stead when he comes face to face with the dark powers that threaten him on and below the earth. For where the proud, pampered, princely stallion may fail, the little un-sightly old mare, tattered as she looks, will find a way, for her whole life has been spent battling for existence on behalf of her foal with cunning and endurance and her kind of courage. In her and the likes of her are personified the centuries of common sense, ingenuity, instinctive knowledge, and the capacity to abide, to weather the storm, without which mankind in the lean land of Connemara could never have survived, and could not survive today.

For Connemara is a mountainous tract of land, unrewarding in terms of conven-tional agriculture, reaching out to sea between Galway and Westport. On both sides the Atlantic frets away at the coastline, its waves crashing against the cliffs. Behind it two long loughs of fresh water make a barrier between itself and the rest of Ireland.

The landscape of this 'island' is full of lakes and tarns and ponds, in and out of which flow numerous streams and rivers, on their way to the sea.

This landscape of the Twelve Bens country is often bathed in enchanting pastel shades, with dark violet mountains, soft green meadows and slopes, the water below them and the sky above a delicate pale blue, with the land reflected in the water and the clouds spreading across the sky, chased by Atlantic winds.

The colours change in a moment, and on such an evening when the skies were beginning to darken we were driving through a countryside that seemed petrified. Nothing but stone all about us: rocks on the strand, rocks in the meadows, below the rocky slopes of the mountains. A single white horse appeared like a ghost, then a rain-

Sparkling eyes and a vigilant look proclaim the stamp of freedom.

While the youngsters play and romp, the mares stand muzzle to muzzle or scratch each other's hides.

The stony pastures stretch along the sea-coast like a landscape from the primeval world.

With the caution born of long practice, this mare snatches a bite from a deep cranny.

The foals of this country are confident and sturdy little creatures.

The ass has also been domiciled here for some centuries.

Flight—
feigned or
real? Over
the hill at a
gallop.

bedraggled troop of horses by the roadside. A dun mare came picking her way down the scree, her albino foal at foot, crossing the road in front of the car to nibble at the sedges on the verge of the bog.

Next morning the air was as clear as glass. Hardly a cloud in the sky, out of which the sun shone brilliantly on every stick and stone and living creature: the dew glittered on the green meadows, making with the deep blue of water and sky and the rust-red mosses on the rocks a satiety of colour. Along the horizon the mountains showed brown and purple, and all this Northern scene seemed lit by a Mediterranean clarity, as of some antique painting. The Twelve Bens towered up, conical wedges of quartzite, little more than 2300 feet high, yet impinging on the Continental eye like the glittering Dolomites, with their incomparably fantastic shapes and harmonious symmetry, brought down to sea-level.

In a moment the white clouds can turn black. The west wind brings great masses of moisture with it. The mean annual rainfall of 250 cm. mostly descends on Connemara in the form of drizzle or sea-fret or short showers.

In the rain, the landscape reveals further, more melancholy charm. The eye is drawn to the dark-brown peat-hags, their edges chequered with the mark of turf spades, their feet in a broth of brown earth, scattered over the bog. Blocks of turf, piled loosely to dry in the wind, soak up more moisture as rivulets burst out from the hillside and the ground makes a sucking sound underfoot.

But it seldom rains for long. Often the drizzle gives way to drifts of mist, which rise thinly from the rocks and the slate-grey surface of the lakes and ponds, hanging spectrally about the hills and the few trees.

We are on the lookout for horses. . . .

Our way lies between rocky hills, and broad, shallow bays, and all the time we battle against the wind as it tears at our clothing. Strong it is, and fresh, but not cold.

We plod patiently onward among primeval rocks. Foals sport together on the crest of a hill before us, and are gone in a flash. Made keener by the sight, we clamber up-

9

ward among boulders washed smooth by the rain and painted with the tiny yellow bloom of lichens.

The herd is grazing in a shallow hollow, on short, stiff grass. To our left is a glint of the sea, while on the right the bog is seamed with tall iris flowers in harsh tones of mauve and orange.

A chestnut, a few bays, many greys of all shades, they graze in widely scattered formation, among them a white mare at sight of which one understands why the Gaels who lived here twenty-five centuries ago peopled their fairyland with magic white horses. This landscape and these horses have changed little since that day. The stone walls look like dragons slowly crawling across the ground—like giant reptiles that have come up out of the sea, with moss on their backs.

And the herds graze in freedom.

The youngsters romp and play, shying at a puff of wind or a stray dog or our shadows. A group of fillies stand preening themselves, in the sun's warmth, standing muzzle to muzzle, nibbling the twitching hide of each other's necks. Mares heavy in foal quarter the ground for titbits, and find the herb they sought sprouting in a cleft of rock, thrusting their muzzles cautiously between the sharp-edged stones.

We force our way through knee-high rushes. Water squelches underfoot. The mares keep their eye on us, and move away, still grazing, as we approach. At last the click of camera shutters scares them into a gallop, and over the skyline they go; there is no fence that will hold them.

Freedom in the windy wilderness—how narrow the pastures, how dull the air of inland places must seem to these ponies, creatures of the wind.

Yet even here limits are set to their wandering. They are loosely confined by stone walls. Stone is of the essence of Galway, and where in other countries men have felled trees and cut posts and rails for fences, here the farmer sets stone on stone to hedge his fields, as he always has done. Many of them are overgrown with brambles that bind them together, others have crumbled and tumbled with the years, and have been replaced by a new wall a few yards distant, while they fade back into the same scree that once they were. Bracken climbs over them, crumbs of earth blow into the cracks, grass and bog plants take root there, until gradually the old wall provides grazing for horses. . . . Year after year the foals have to pick their way through this maze of sharp stone, thorn bushes, and fetlock-deep adhesive swamp, so that even at a few days old they are as light-footed as ballerinas, putting down their feet with instinctive sureness, and tearing off at a gallop, over ground where we totter painfully forward step by step.

No wonder that such foals grow into horses that make no bones about the going in the hunting-field, giving the rider that confidence in jumping the massive stone walls which makes the chase of the elusive hare in the west of Ireland such an unforgettable experience.

After some days we found horses even in the place where in all my travels I had never seen any before: down on the strand below high-water mark, among the sea-tangle and the ware, on the bright yellow, glittering, slippery mud. Here, where sea-grass grows on the rocks like delicate hair, waving in the wind like the dun manes of the ponies, here among the exposed acres of bladderwrack, they munch their favourite seaweed, rich in iodine and mineral trace-elements.

The landscape has set its mark on these ponies, as all landscapes do. But what is the characteristic stamp of Connemara, as seen at home? Where the Atlantic wind plays in manes and tails, where the broad sky is reflected in their bright eyes, where treacherous bog and morass teach caution, and slippery loose stones teach sure-footedness the hard way, where nature generation after generation has remorselessly practised selection, a type has been evolved, peculiar to this environment alone; it is of medium size, and tough, with strong joints, hard feet, iron constitution, utter reliability, and a clear, 'windswept' style of beauty which is marked by a certain appearance of mane and tail and winter coat, that reminds one of moss and reeds and sea-ware!

The history of these ponies goes back to remote antiquity. Recent research has established the probability that they are descended from that variety of wild horse which in prehistoric times inhabited Western Europe north of the 50th degree of latitude, and is therefore closely related to the ponies of Scandinavia, Iceland, Shetland, and Great Britain. But it is also certain that, unusually early after domestication, southern strains were added to the Irish horse-stock.

This is connected with a geographical peculiarity of Ireland, and particularly of the west coast. Ocean currents and prevailing winds at certain seasons make direct traffic between here and Northern Spain easier than with other parts of the Continent. This route was used by Mediterranean traders long before the Christian era, and there have been many waves of human settlement reaching Ireland from the Mediterranean by sea.

In the sixth century B.C. the Celts broke out of the Lower Danube valley and overran the whole of Europe as far as the Atlantic and North Sea coasts. Horses and horsebreeding played an important part in the lives of this Indo-European people, and contact both by means of raiding and trading with the Balkans, the Black Sea region, and Asia Minor will have made available to them a great variety of horses, including the ancestors of what we now call the Arabian.

Typical were the wanderings of the Brigantes [the Bregenzerwald at the far end of Lake Constance, in Vorarlberg, the smallest Austrian province, was once the *Silva Brigantium*—the Forest of the Brigantes—and the town of Bregenz on the lake shore is named after them. *Tr.*]. So also was the place we know as Coruña in Spanish Galicia— it too was known in Roman times as Brigantium. From there they took ship and coasted along the shores of the Bay of Biscay, then sailed across the mouth of the Channel and entered the Irish Sea. Part of the Brigantes settled in the North of England, another part in County Waterford. During their sojourn in Galicia, on the Atlantic coast of Spain, their territory bordered on that of the Asturians. These two provinces, Galicia and Asturias, had in antiquity some renown as the home of a distinctive breed of horse, called *asturcones*; light, fast, good-looking pacing ponies, between which and the war-horse of Southern Spain, the Andalusian, such authors as Pliny already distinguish; it is quite possible, however, that before the time of the

The Celtic Pony of today in all its wind-blown, dishevelled beauty.

The foals grow up in paddocks divided by drystone walls . . .

. . . cutting them off from the cultivated land.

The walls provide windbreaks on stormy days.

Masses of bladderwrack grow below the high-tide mark . . .

. . . together with yellow sea-grass fine as human hair . . .

. . . it waves in the wind like the ponies' manes.

As much at home among the seaweed and slime of the ebb as on dry land.

Brigantian resettlement the large war-horse of the south was being crossed, in Spain, with the Galician–Asturian pacer, and perhaps even with Barbs from North Africa. A large part of the Roman garrison of Great Britain consisted of cavalry recruited in Spain and mounted on Spanish horses. Ireland, never occupied by the Romans, had access to exactly the same source of stock, though it was put to slightly different uses. The war-chariot, obsolescent in Britain at the time of the first Roman invasion, was still an essential institution of the Irish heroic society, among the Brigantes as among the other Gaels of Hibernia, until the time of St Patrick.

From that time onward there followed many centuries of trade with the Iberian peninsula, whereby large numbers of horses, both from there and from Barbary, made their way into Ireland through the harbours of the west coast. By comparison with this, the isolated instance of the mythical stallion swimming ashore from an Armada galleon in September 1588 would be insignificant even if it were true, which it demonstrably is not. About the middle of the last century some landowning families imported Arab stallions, which may have had their influence one way or another. No-one is in a position to say to what extent their progeny, together with that of the Barbs and the Andalusians, were able to survive the storms and the cold winter rains in the bogs and the hills of Connemara, with only the indigestible winter grazing as provender. These are all dry-climate horses. The Galician, on the other hand, came from an Atlantic climate much more akin to that of Galway. It is impossible to express proportionately how much of their blood has remained in the Connemara of today, but if colour is any guide, and if yellow dun can be taken as the hallmark of the original 'northern' element, this is greatly outnumbered by greys of all shades, a colour regarded as typical of the 'southern' imports. As to conformation, it is not difficult for the amateur of Arabs and Barbs to pick out points in the individual pony strongly reminiscent of these breeds.

The fact that Connemara was the most remote and backward part of the most remote and backward province has contributed, as in so many other instances, to the 'purity' of the breed. As the autonomous Irish rulers during the centuries of struggle, first with the Norse and then with the Anglo–Normans, were pushed farther and farther west, so the native 'hobby' which they rode in preference to the Anglo–Norman 'great horse' also shifted its centre of gravity farther west. The final solution under Cromwell—"to Hell or Connaught"—had its reality in terms of horses as well as of men. And so "like everything else of native design, the curragh, the costumes, the bards, the harpers, the cattle-thieves, etc., the native pony was pushed farther and farther west from the times of Essex and Cromwell onward"[1] until finally it vanished into the bogs and the hills and valleys of this most Irish part of Ireland, where it was more or less forgotten by the outside world. . . .

Life and Work in Connemara

Here in the far West the ponies were put to manifold tasks. Of these unquestionably the most important was pack-work, for there were few vehicles, and the small farm-steads lay far apart.

"A two-year-old filly having been purchased," we read in a description at the end of the last century, "a bridle is soon woven out of horse-hair, and a primitive pack saddle constructed out of four pieces of wood. The only additional furniture needed are mats or sacks to place under the saddle, and a cushion or pillion for the hind quarters on which the owner sits on the way to market. Horse-hair or ordinary ropes hold the various trappings. The work varies with the season of the year. At one time they may be seen climbing steep hillsides heavily laden with seaweed, seed corn, or potatoes; at another they convey the produce to market. Sometimes it is a load of turf, oats, or barley; at other times creels crowded with a lively family of young pigs. During summer and autumn the ponies are often seen trudging unsteadily along, all but buried in a huge pile of hay or oats, each with a puzzled foal thoughtfully bringing

[1] *The Foals of Epona*, by A. Dent and Daphne Goodall (Galley Press, 1962).

up the rear. Returning from market each pony generally carries two men, one in front and the other on the pillion. A good pony can easily carry two men thus disposed for a considerable distance at the rate of ten miles an hour. The women seem quite as much at home on the pillion as the men."

The few visitors who in the nineteenth century went touring through distant Connemara described with some astonishment the strings of ponies which they met, laden with peat or reeds for thatching, and the nice sense of balance which they displayed as they tripped along the rough, steep mountain tracks, carrying a boy or girl behind the load, who guided them with nothing but a stick. Mrs B. Pattison wrote in the *Temple Bar Magazine* in 1896: "We saw one girl make her pony kneel down while she sprang up behind her creels" [on Achill Island].

Loud were the praises of the gentle temperament, the robust health, and the endurance of these ponies. Thomas Meleady, a Dublin horse-dealer, in evidence before the Royal Commission of 1897, deposed, *inter alia*, as follows: "When I went down there first [*c.* 1860?] there was a breed of ponies in it you could get up and ride them off the grass thirty miles across the mountains as I often did from Belmullet into Ballina, and they would never tire, without a feed of oats, nor did they know what the taste of oats was. . . ."

Another time we hear of a 16-year-old pony that had never worn a bridle being requisitioned by a surveyor laying out a new road in the West in the 1700's. William Youatt quotes the surveyor, one Pinkerton. The unaccustomed live weight on his back caused the pony no alarm, but when he came to a really dangerous spot he would not take a step farther down the steep and stony slope: "The reasoning process in his mind was evident enough, and often amused me afterwards. 'You may have your whims when you cannot do either yourself or myself much harm, but I do not choose to risk my neck for you or anyone.' The bridle was taken off, he selected his own path, and the rider was taken over an exceedingly dangerous heap of rocks, with a degree of caution which I could not help admiring in the midst of my terror."

Some ponies were bred west of Galway that were supposed to have Barb blood. Another witness before the 1897 Royal Commission, Mr Ussher, said of them: "They were without exception the best animals I ever knew—good shoulders, good hard legs, good action, great stamina, they were seldom over 14 hands two inches. I never knew one of them to have a spavin or a splint, or to be in any respect unsound in his wind." Another eye-witness described the Connemaras of his time as "long and low, with good rein, good back and well-coupled", and concluded, "I never saw lovelier mares." (Quoted by Sir Walter Gilbey, 1900.)

But even then laments were heard—Jeremiahs foretelling the demise of the good old breed. The famines of the Hungry Forties had brought the farmers (who were poor enough anyway) to such straits that they were forced to sell their mares.

In the 1860's and 1870's polo had just been introduced to 'home stations' by officers returning from service in India. At that time all British native ponies were quite adequate in size for polo-players, since the ponies used for this purpose in India had been very diminutive indeed. There was a brisk trade for some decades in Connemara ponies for polo-players; five-year-olds at £16 or £18, exceptionally for as much as £30. But by the end of the century the trend was towards taller ponies (originally for part-bred Arabs), and Connemara lost this market—not inevitably but by oversight. The part-Arab in its turn was replaced by the pony with a great deal of TB blood, and subsequently by the Argentine *criollo*, as the height limit for polo was successively raised more and more, and finally abolished altogether. It would have been quite possible to breed polo ponies to all these later specifications using Connemara or half-Connemara brood mares, but for one reason or another this did not happen.

The specialized demand for children's ponies did not exist by that date, and the only outlet was to the richer agricultural areas in the south and east of Ireland. The only solution for the poor Galway farmer with a few brood mares was to try to produce 'agricultural' horses from them by putting them to larger stallions. To this end the Government distributed gratis Clydesdale colts which were surplus to Scottish

The bogs and the banks of streams provide a varied diet.

Moycullen Dan (226) by Dun Aengus (120) out of Muffy (2157) asserts his authority.

Something has alarmed the mares, so Moycullen Dan rounds them up.

Evening falls on lonely Connemara . . .

. . . and a fine drizzle blurs the outlines of mountains and trees.

An old dun mare comes down the scree, her albino foal at foot. . . .

. . . She and another cross the road, oblivious of the rain . . .

. . . to seek out some herb among the rushes on the lake-shore.

requirements. This gave quick and disastrous results. The matings indeed produced larger foals, which inherited along with other 'cold-blood' characteristics that of early maturity (one of the attributes shared by the native pony of North-west Europe and the hot-blooded light horse of the South is late maturity). These cross-breds had height but no substance. They had thick but soft bone below the knee, and much hair on the fetlocks. Meleady said of them "The mixture of ponies with Scotch horses that got into Galway and County Mayo ruined that country, and they are neither horses nor ponies . . . soft, hairy-legged bits of ponies, and no use." The Government in London now tried to rectify matters by sending out Thoroughbred, Hunter, and Hackney stallions; those of their progeny that survived were indeed of riding type— but what proportion survived? These ill-conceived efforts at 'improvement' were severely controlled by the very nature of the country. In that rain-soaked environment the mares had either to work off the grass or pick up a living for their foals and themselves on the mountain, and natural selection based on the ability to survive the winters came into play. An expert (Bernard O'Sullivan) has written: "We have yet to meet a specimen of the Thoroughbred, Half-bred, Hackney or Clydesdale capable of living through a winter in a valley of the Twelve Pins, relying on some convenient rock or hillock for shelter from the blast."

In the more fertile marginal areas of Connemara the influence of these exotic stallions was so strong that the good old breed became extinct, and no trace of it survives to this day.

The Survey

One result of the 1897 Commission was that in 1900 Professor T. Cossar Ewart of Edinburgh was invited to make a survey of the Connemara pony-breeding region. His report is the most informative document on the breeding of riding ponies known to me, and I can do no better than quote from it *in extenso*, with a few abridgements, letting this percipient and knowledgeable man speak for himself.

"There are nowhere else, so far as I know", he says, "in the British Islands, ponies with so much stamina as those I have included in the Clifden Section." He commends their bone and substance, the strength of their backs, which can take practically any load. He was deeply impressed also by their light-footedness, their intelligence and docility, and by their capacity for work "under conditions which would speedily prove disastrous to horses reared under less natural conditions".

He goes very exactly into the reasons for this excellence; the topography of Connemara presents a great variety, mountains of different heights alternating with small plateaux and valleys. There is abundance of water, in the form of bogs, interspersed with streams, rivers, and irregularly shaped lakes, which cut up the country into small parcels. The grazings are often only a few feet above sea-level, and the whole provides an adequate and suitable grazing territory for many separate breeding herds.

But the climate is even more significant than the conformation of the land. Mean annual temperatures in Connemara are comparable with those of Southern Europe. Summer nights 7°C., midday 15°C.; but also winter nights 7° and winter meridional 15°! The virtual absence of night frost is due to the Gulf Stream, whose waters flow up the countless indentations of the long coastline, and from the surface of the sea warm breezes blow over the land most of the year. Temperature and humidity have a combined effect on the vegetable growth: grasses, herbs, and all kinds of mountain plants, mosses, reeds, rushes, and the like begin to sprout early in the year, keeping fresh and green all summer, and retaining much of their nutrient value through the winter. This is the reason for the comparatively great height of the Connemara pony. If the average is 13 hands, 14 hands is by no means uncommon.

The quality of the soil out of which these plants grow is also of importance. The slopes of Connemara mountains mostly consist of weathered archaic rocks, while the floors of the valleys contain limestone as well as beds of clay: the whole is geologically rich in phosphates, potash, and carboniferous soils. Moreover, the irregularity of the surface, cut up by narrow valleys, steep slopes, stretches of salt and fresh water and swamp, makes it unsuitable for arable farming, and imposes a virtual monopoly for pastoral economy.

The climate, the richness of the soil (by certain standards), and the geological formation, taken together, provide an unusually favourable setting for the breeding of tough, active, powerful ponies of about the same stature as those which in the New World were such a common feature of the Great Plains and Rocky Mountain regions, as of the pampas and llanos below the Equator; of much the same stature also as those half-wild herds which still survive in Central Asia and Mongolia.

Free range implies also free choice of grazing. These ponies have retained the urge derived from the wild horse to select hard, fibrous food-plants at certain seasons. In temperate zones the natural inclination of the horse is to prefer hard shrubs and heaths to the tough and apparently tasteless winter grass, or what is left of it. During the exhausting period when vital energy is being expended on the change of coat, it is common to see wild ponies browsing on broom, heather, and such hard fodder. If their pastures do not contain such vegetation they will gnaw bark from trees (preferably birch-trees), or dig up roots and devour them. Some individuals will prefer heather, broom, or furze, while others strip bark or scrape up roots. Ewart continues:

"In a mixed herd of Equidae some prefer gorse and heaths, others as readily take to bark and the smaller branches of fallen trees, while others direct their attention to underground stems. Recently I came upon a mixed family, all in excellent condition, busily engaged digging up and eating, apparently with great relish, the underground stems of nettles. Not far from this group some hybrids were cutting off and devouring branches (over an inch in circumference) of a fallen beech tree, and in an adjoining paddock several ponies, instead of feeding on the excellent hay provided, were directing their attention to the fences. In Shetland the ponies are said to consume seaweeds, while in Iceland, when the usually scanty supply of hay comes to an end, they readily take to eating cods' heads specially reserved for them during the fishing season.

"It might be said that in the case of the domestic horse the instinct to feed on shrubs, underground stems, branches, leaves, etc., might well have been allowed to lapse. It should, however, be borne in mind that without this instinct thousands of horses in Europe and a countless number in Africa and Asia would annually perish, and that our semi-wild ponies probably owe their hardiness and their freedom from various diseases largely to their feeding on shrubs and other fibrous substances during the interval between winter and spring. Without a wide range or frequent change of pasture, it is difficult to rear vigorous hardy horses; but the wild herbs and the dwarf shrubs that occur so plentifully on uncultivated moors and uplands, may be quite as essential during colthood as a free and unfettered existence."

Those countries which have 'special relationships' with territories overseas have always had a more basic understanding of the value of ponies than the inward-looking non-colonial Powers of Central Europe, purely because all over the world their merchants, settlers, officials, and administrators have come in contact with a variety of useful and attractive small breeds which were essential to colonial life before the introduction of the motor-car.

In the history of the domestic horse as a whole, the very large horse has, by and large, played a small part, both numerically and economically. Virtually unknown before the Middle Ages, it was deliberately bred up with the sole aim in view of mounting the heavily armoured knight in battle. But once the battle was over, the knight changed horses, mounting his much smaller palfrey, which gave a more comfortable ride for travelling and hunting, while the great war-horse was led in hand by the mounted squire until required for the next action. The invention of firearms put an end to the usefulness of cavalry of this type, and the very large horse was restricted in use to processional functions (as the 'horse of state') in small numbers, the bulk of them being transferred to agricultural use in those countries which had abandoned ox-traction in the plough. This last phase of its employment is now drawing to a close. In the sixteenth century a start was made at breeding light horses taller; this was achieved by hand-feeding and housing all the year round, and the larger specimens

Brought down off the mountain, kept up and groomed for a few days . . .

. . . often
elaborately got up
with braided plaits,
they appear at the
show.

This is Ireland, so
naturally His
Reverence exhibits
his yearling in
person.

Yearling colts at Clifden Show . . .

. . . with a background of four of the twelve Bens.

Greaney Rebel (186) by Inver Rebel (93) out of Nansin Ban (1858); many times a winner, in stallion classes.

Atlantic Mist (2175), a mare by Carna Bobby (79) out of Callowfeenis Dolly II (1913).
Twelve years old, she has won premiums, as a brood mare.

Marble (254), a two-year-old colt by Rebel Wind (127) out of Callowfeenis Dolly II (1913), very gay, and strong indeed for a two-year-old.

so produced eventually replaced the descendants of the medieval war-horse for 'display' purposes, among the upper classes. They were also used, and still are used, for competitive racing and show-jumping. The English with their concentration on practical values were only marginally concerned with the production of larger horses, in spite of the fact that they 'invented' the Thoroughbred. But even the Thoroughbred was bred up from Oriental stock which at the time of original imports was only an average 14 hands high. Intensive feeding, protection from the weather, and selective breeding have produced an increase in height in the blood horse of about a hand every century. Apart from this, the English preserved the 'native' breeds, and from them produced a range of cobs, roadsters, and the like, of the order of 14 or 15 hands, more or less of pony type. These combined with handiness the ability to carry a big man across country, and to live out for at least a part of the year.

It is therefore not surprising that the Scottish Professor Ewart in his report on the Connemara Pony tackled the question of utility, contrasting the pony with the full-sized horse:

"Size, uniformity, shapeliness and fine action are excellent, indeed indispensible in horses taking part in pageants and in park parades, as well as horses harnessed to well appointed carriages. But in the small horses by which the world's work is mainly done endurance, hardiness, nimbleness, intelligence, and docility count for infinitely more than make or action, good looks, or a long pedigree. Make, docility, intelligence, and speed are largely a matter of inheritance, while hardiness and endurance are mainly the products of their surroundings.

"It is for this reason that active and hardy horses are found in the less barren uplands of nearly all sub-tropical areas, and that degenerate forms are often met with in certain parts of India, and areas within the tropics where conditions are unsuitable." He then quotes the opinion of Sir Richard Green-Price, then President of the Polo Pony Society, the justice of which he took for granted, though it seems incredible to us, reading it seventy years later. "Ponies beat moderate horses of double their size", under active service conditions, having "twice the constitution and thrice the sense". [The explanation is that this judgment was passed in the light of conditions obtaining in the South African War, unique conditions which were not to be repeated in the history of the British Army during the few remaining decades during which it had to rely on 'hide-and-hair' cavalry. *Tr.*].

"Large horses are highly specialized products of artificial selection, quite incapable of maintaining themselves in adverse circumstances. Nature makes short work of large horses, and in a few generations mercifully reduces to the pony standard any offspring they may happen to leave." So wrote Ewart in 1900.

It had become apparent, as one of the lessons of the South African War, that in future consideration must be given to the supply of tough, handy ponies that could be used as remounts. A writer in the *Scottish Farmer* expressed the view that great tracts of cheap marginal grazing in a climate that made hand-feeding superfluous in winter would be necessary, together with a foundation stock of hardy, useful, middle-sized mares. The rougher the ground was, the better.

"Grazing among rocks and bogs makes the animals active, sure-footed, and clever in extricating themselves from tight places, a very essential thing for mounted infantry."[1]

The Mounted Infantry that never was

The Ewart memorandum, which contains so much that is valuable for us today, informs us that in 1900 the minimum height requirement for mounted infantry remounts was 13 hands. That is, animals which in some highly sophisticated countries are today regarded as 'children's ponies' were judged capable of campaigning with the weight of a British soldier, his weapons, and equipment, which together will have weighed something like 18 stone (according to how much ammunition was carried) by a

[1] *Scottish Farmer*, April 20th, 1901.

responsible department of the War Office. "If Connemara mares are crossed with hard, useful, unspoilt Thoroughbreds, then doubtless the progeny will be suitable for light cavalry and just the size (14 to 15½ hands) that has proved itself in this war hard enough and handy enough to withstand campaigning conditions."

The memorandum concluded with a proposal to make Connemara into a sort of giant stud-farm that would produce a considerable crop of foals every year. At weaning, these were to run on the hills until the time came to break them in, whereby they would bring to their future employment a constitution that would defy all normal hardships of active service.

"The only danger would be that by rich food, much grooming and warm stables they would ere long be as delicate as ponies reared in the ordinary way. All that healthy, hardy ponies require is shelter from wind and rain. A shed completely open on one side, but with a wide roof is sufficient; but at several centres a sort of equine Pantheon, with or without galleries, might be constructed to serve as winter quarters."

[Never mind the fact that this plan never materialized: notoriously the War Office is always admirably prepared to fight the last war (or the last war but one). The peculiar conditions of the South African War were never encountered again; an enemy so weak in numbers, so highly skilled in marksmanship and horsemanship, or so admirably mounted as the Boers, was never encountered before the First World War, in which masses of conventionally mounted British cavalry spent months on end manning trenches on the Western Front (or rather four-fifths of them did; every fifth man was kept back in the horse-lines, grooming and feeding the horses and doing no harm to the enemy). Otherwise cavalry were simply standing by in the back areas, waiting for the breakthrough which never came, while far away in Palestine a British mounted army did indeed operate brilliantly against the Turks; but it consisted very largely of Australian and New Zealand cavalry, mounted on horses much more like, in size and conformation, the hunter or hack type from which they were derived. *Tr.*].

Even if Connemara did not become one great remount farm, it is worth substituting, in the mind's eye, the grown-up civilian leisure-horseman of today for the mounted infantryman of Ewart's dreams, and considering how the type of general-utility riding-horse that it was proposed to breed on a large scale in Connemara would have suited his needs.

Three proposals arose out of the investigation. Ewart advised the Government:

(*i*) to seek out the best available stallions among the Connemara ponies and to concentrate them in covering-stations, such as we now have for bulls;

(*ii*) to open a register of pure-bred Connemara mares, thus laying the foundations of a future Stud Book;

(*iii*) to induce the farmers actually to use the selected stallions.

Implementation of the Report

Nothing was done about all this well-considered advice until 1914. There then ensued the First World War, the Anglo–Irish War, and the Irish Civil War, the echoes of which did not die away until 1922. [Note that the popular British and Irish view of every war is that it will be 'over by Christmas'. As it takes a minimum of five years to breed and make a troop-horse, obviously it was not worth the while of the British Government, or its successor the infant Free State Government, to initiate such a re-mount plan. *Tr.*]. But in 1923 the Connemara Pony Breeders' Society was founded in Galway with the backing of the Department of Agriculture. Its first meeting resolved measures which very closely reflected the proposals of the Ewart memorandum, with entirely civilian ends in view. They were:

(*i*) to improve the breed 'from within', by the best selection from available local stock;

(*ii*) to select some hundred mares, of the desired type, and a suitable number of stallions of the same type, as foundation stock;

(*iii*) to request the help of the appropriate Government department to provide funds for the purchase of the best stallions, and to grant subsidies to owners of suitable mares for the payment of stud fees to these stallions.

The type to be aimed at was defined as follows: ponies of iron constitution, toughness, endurance, intelligence, and kindness, between 13 and 14 hands, with a compact but rather long body, short, powerful legs, a riding shoulder and a long neck with a fine head, well set on. The legs should be dry, with plenty of bone below the knee (about 8 or 9 inches round), with an ample stride but not too flat an action; colours to be grey, black, brown, bay, and dun (occasional chestnut and roan is allowable, but must not occur too often).

These were the criteria for a painstaking selection. Vol. 1 of the *Stud Book*, printed in 1926, lists 93 mares and nine stallions, each individually inspected by a committee, who measured and tried them. The strict rules are still in force today. Although the *Stud Book* was closed in 1964, and thenceforward barred to those ponies without both parents registered, the committee still has the right of personal inspection to determine whether the young horse is of sufficiently pronounced type to be entered in the book and allotted a number.

To date eleven volumes of the book have been issued, between 1926 and 1967, registering about 3000 mares and 200 stallions. The committee's job was not easy, for—as we have seen—in the not too remote past much alien blood had been introduced. The problem was to breed this out. But it was amazing, over the years, to see what a wealth of good mares of the old stamp was forthcoming from the inner fastnesses of the Connemara hill country.

An example of this unsuspected wealth came to light while the committee were touring a remote valley among the Twelve Bens, where a farmer in rather poor circumstances produced seven young mares, six of which were good enough to register. When asked, the farmer revealed that he had as many good mares again where they came from, only he had not brought them up as he had not been able to catch them!

Nobody would have suspected him of owning more than one cow and one horse—but in fact he possessed a valuable breeding herd. He had no arable ground to speak of, but like many another mountain farmer he took full advantage of his rights in the common grazings, and kept brood mares. He had never yet shown one, and these six might never have seen the light of day had not the committee sought them out.

So it came about that for nearly forty years mares were constantly coming forward for inspection, and many were registered. The stallion situation was not nearly so satisfactory. It had for too long been the local practice to sell off colts at the first opportunity, and only to keep the fillies. Now and again a colt escaped the round-up, grew up 'living rough' in the mountains, and was used to cover the mares (or rather, no-one stopped him covering the mares). Not much time was spent on such matters, and there was no question of a long-term breeding policy.

The efforts of the Connemara Breeders' Society are directed towards producing a pony of uniform type. The best mares are covered gratis by good stallions, and premiums are given for the best foals. In order to improve the standard of stallions, the Society buys every autumn ten or twelve foals, and turns them out on a rough mountain pasture. During occasional winter frosts or snowfalls they live on broom, furze, and similar browsing. Exceptionally they are fed hay, but never brought up. By this means the weaklings are soon sorted out. At the age of two and a half they are inspected by the committee.

The society has lately formed the intention of buying a suitable farm on which to rear the colts; there, too, the mature stallions which they own will spend the winters; all will be broken to saddle by a competent horsemaster. The latter service will also be available for members' colts.

In the matter of coat-colour, grey of all shades predominates, with more than 50 per cent of registered animals. Blacks are slightly more frequent than bay or brown (most of the browns are dark dun rather than dark bay), and the golden dun colour with black mane and black points, once so characteristic of the old-fashioned sort, seems unfortunately to be on the wane. Some duns mated with a white horse produce albinos (politely called 'blue-eyed creams') which are not popular; so does the mating of white with chestnut. The albino, with its insipid appearance, is only tolerated as an inevitable by-product of the much-desired palomino, which can arise from the same mating. There are in fact very few chestnuts—this colour is not regarded as typical, and breeders do not like it.

All in all the measures of the last forty years have saved this fine old breed from extinction or degeneration.

The Shop-window

Annually in August the great Clifden Show takes place. Of course there are Connemara classes—more and more of them—at the great international Summer Show at Dublin, and they are well filled; but there they tend to get lost in the mass, whereas at Clifden everything revolves round them. Clifden is the meeting-place of local breeders and of connoisseurs of the breed from all over the world. It is a turbulent, hectic day dominated by a figure from the past, risen phoenix-like from the ashes— the 'shaggy old pony' of legend [the 'Shan Bui' interpreted by Somerville and Ross in 1906 as 'the name we has in this country for them yella horses with the black sthripe on their back'. *Tr.*].

Clifden is picturesquely sited on cliffs above the sea; the population is nine hundred, with two churches and seven pubs—a sleepy and charming fishing village with a back-drop of the Twelve Bens; what a German guide-book writer calls "an oasis of divine content amidst primeval rock and mountain". The rock walls are overgrown with fuchsia and rhododendron, the sands below the cliff are white and firm. The surrounding district is a favourite one with painters and those who seek solitude, fishing or boating or snipe-shooting, with only the wind in the cliffs and the flocks of seagulls for company.

The hotel is a babel of many tongues, and it is well to book one's accommodation for Show Day the year before. In the bar the talk is all of ponies. There are buyers from overseas or from Scandinavia, Holland, Germany, importuning the local experts for inside information. For three days and nights the quiet atmosphere proper to poets and philosophers is shattered by the din of rowdy, congenial horse-fanciers.

The Great Day passes off in a way so typically Irish that the foreign visitor had better get rid of all preconceived notions from the start. It is no use sallying forth on the eve of the show to get a preview of the assembled exhibits. You can wander through the pastures around the village, up and down the lanes and the alleys, and stick your nose into everything that looks like a stable—and go back to the hotel without having glimpsed hide or hair. At nine the following morning the main street is still deserted. The show-ground beside a sparkling, babbling little river presents a scene of amiable chaos; workmen are laying cable for the loudspeaker, knocking up a stage for Irish folk-dances, fitting shelves on which will be displayed competitive samples of home-made jam, home-grown peas, home-knitted sweaters, and suchlike examples of domestic industry, while the rain-clouds gather in the sky.

And never a pony in sight.

The band turns up shortly before ten o'clock, followed by the judges. And at eleven the first pony class begins. All of a sudden they materialize. They come down the slopes of the mountain in herds, they pour out of horse-boxes and trailers, they fill the main street with the clatter of their neat hooves, they prance out of every alleyway, to mingle instantly with the flood of spectators who are simultaneously converging on the show-ground. The deep voices of the mares fill the air, answered by the high-pitched whicker of foals who have been parted from their dams by the press of traffic or their own curiosity. Brushes and rubbers and sponges are plied, and every member of the family puts a finishing touch to the exhibit which stands patiently in the midst of the turmoil. The great show is set in motion as if by the touch of a magician. Here are Press and television, guest of honour, cameramen, reporters; from now until the

Murrisk (217) by MacDara (91) out of Grey Girl (2021), the Lord of the Herd . . .

. . . never takes his eye off the mares, as they draw to the shade of an old tree . . .

. . . or the
foals,
inquisitively
exploring the
verges of their
little world . . .

. . . and all his family, dreaming away the summer day.

Connemara pony, as young girls' hack-hunter.

Clonkeehan Maypole, a gelding by the Arab Naseel out of Rose of Barna (1337), elegantly turned out for the International Show at Dublin. (*Independent Newspapers*)

Connemara mare taking a ditch very big in a cross-country course. (Sally Ann by Carna Bobby (29) out of Starlight (1122).) (*Reed, Tring.*)

The gelding Dundrum by the TB Little Heaven out of Evergood (1945).
A champion jumper of world renown as 'the little horse with the big heart'.

(Irish Times, Dublin)

evening there is one round of judging, feasting, talking, dealing, and swopping. Friends meet each other, dealers scent a customer in the wind, connoisseurs are invited to come up the mountain and see the rest of the herd; ponies bedecked with sashes and rosettes come out of the ring.

So it has been, year after year. The only thing that has changed is the standard of type and condition, steadily improving for reasons that lie far outside the bounds of Connemara.

Pony Type

For a definition of what makes a pony, as opposed to a small horse, I must turn again to Ewart, who distinguished between 'true' and 'false' ponies. By the former he means principally those breeds of North-western Europe whose ancestors came out of the Eurasian land-mass in post-glacial times, during which migration they suffered a dwarfing process which affected less the depth of the body than the proportionate length of the legs, especially in the insular and coastal regions of the North Atlantic. 'False' ponies, on the other hand, are the part-bred descendants of the larger domestic breeds crossed with 'true' ponies, or else feral ponies wholly derived from larger domestic stock which in the process of 'going wild' again have lost height.

This is more definite than any attempt to define a pony in terms of hands and inches or centimetres. But we should bear in mind that the Continental image of a 'poney'— something the size of a Shetland—represents an extreme dwarf form brought about by millennia of acclimatization to a particular environment, and this diminutive stature is untypical of ponies as a whole.

In Connemara, as we have seen, 'authentic' ponies have survived from past ages, and the intention when the Stud Book was founded was to renovate the breed exclusively by having recourse to local stock, 'from within'. Regrettably, this has not proved entirely possible. Probably the motive has been the desire to produce something more elegant and a little larger than the raw material of the mountains. The following exotics were crossed-in: two Thoroughbreds—Winter and Little Heaven; two Irish Draft stallions—Scribbereen and May Boy; one quarter-Welsh-Cob—Cannon Ball; and one Arab—Naseel, represented principally by his son Clonkeehan Auratum. All were much used. Some breed societies outside Ireland, more Catholic than the Pope, exclude the descendants of these 'alien' sires from certain championships. One cannot but wonder what happens when, for instance, a half-Arab mare is put to a half-Arab stallion, or Naseel to one of his own daughters. It would be hard to define the offspring as a Connemara Pony.

Winners of premiums and important show prizes of late years have, however, tended to be pure pony types, such as the entrancingly beautiful grey mare Atlantic Mist (No. 175, by Carna Bobby out of Callowfeenis Dolly). Deep, compact, with short cannon bones and a great second thigh, standing over much ground, with a wonderfully maternal appearance, the image of a brood mare. She has a low-set tail and a rather sloping croup, as has the much-decorated stallion Greaney Rebel (186, by Inver Rebel out of Nansin Ban). This pony has a strikingly pronounced wedge-shaped pony head, and strong legs. Ponies like this are true family horses, able to carry young and old alike.

This is the Connemara pony's long suit. It is sturdy, hardy, handy, almost on the scale of a cob. It is the largest British pony of purely riding type. [This means that the author excludes the Dales and the Highlander. *Tr.*]. Although no pony over 14 hands 2 inches can be registered, and the preferred height is about 13 hands 3 inches, there are unregistered but pure-bred individuals as tall as 15 hands, in some numbers.

European ideas about the horse have been radically revised of late years in regard to size. It is no longer exclusively a matter of 'the High Horse'. Our horizon has widened to take in those breeds which for centuries have carried adults as well as children, in peace and in war, whether into the next parish or half-way round the world. All those types in stature between 13 and $14\frac{1}{2}$ hands have become known and popular with us, as Icelanders, Highlanders, Fell, Dales, New Forest, Fjord, Gudbrandsdal, Haflinger, Duelmen, Carpathian Mountain ponies, Welsh Cobs, as well as Connemara ponies. These are the ponies which have also shared the leisure pursuits of their owners; hunting over stone walls of Ireland or the cut-and-laid fences of England; peasant races in the Tirol and Dalmatia; tilting at the ring and the quintain, and the Central European version of the Gretna Green race; now too they compete at international level, in harness events, at dressage, and show-jumping. There is no more versatile class of horse, combining as they do varied utility with modest requirements in feeding and housing, robust constitution, and equable temperament. If only ten years ago the Society was still having difficulty in persuading the Connemara farmers to follow their line in breeding aims, much has changed meanwhile.

Since then the tide has strongly set in all over the world in favour of ponies, and consequently the demand for Connemara ponies has risen with it. The English Connemara Pony Society was founded in 1946, but before that Connemara ponies were registered in a separate section of the National Pony Society's Stud Book. The first exports to America took place in 1957. And the price of a weaned foal then was £20.

In 1965 there were exports to the following countries: the United States, France, Germany, Belgium, Holland, Denmark, and Sweden. The price of a weaned foal was about £100.

In 1967 Connemara ponies were sent to South Africa and Australia, and exports to other countries rose rapidly, as did the prices. Now some foals were sold for as much as £200 and £300. Money would not buy some of the brood mares (let us hope for the good of Connemara that it never will); untried mares of three and four years old were offered to dumbfounded buyers for £500. That was the asking price on the spot— cash and carry, with all the freight charges to come . . . not to speak of customs dues. The day after Clifden Show in 1968 an Irish journalist asked in print: "How high can a Connemara pony jump—in price?"

It is therefore understandable that the breeders should take more trouble about their stock than once they did, and that the ponies shown at Clifden today are better fed, better cared for, better done in every way, and better bred than ever before.

Round the ring at Clifden, where the judges are looking for pony type as defined above, we have, not just a circle of curious bystanders but a large number of informed breeders and riders, who know what the judges are doing. How else would it be possible for a one-breed show with no ridden classes—only ponies shown in hand of all ages and sexes—to attract such a gate, drawn from all over the world?

There is a continuous buzz of conversation and comment, laced with the registered numbers of brood mares or the pedigree of this or that stallion, or reminiscences of the career of this or that pony.

It has not been easy to impose a unified aim on the breeding of Connemara ponies. [Indeed, the whole conceptions (*a*) of imposition as such and (*b*) of unified aims supervised by Big Brother are somewhat alien to the sympathies of Irish people and pony-breeders anyhow. *Tr.*]. But in any case the worldwide distribution means that different customers have different requirements. Americans want jumping ability and endurance. In their country competitive jumping by teenagers and young adults and trail-riding (trekking) by holiday-makers of all ages is gaining in popularity. The Swedes have principally bought ponies with some Arab blood as good-looking small hacks. The English Connemara Stud Book, now printed independently, is conducted exactly according to the rules of the Galway Stud Book. But there is a considerable market in England for Connemara mares as the basis for the cross-breeding of riding ponies. "Put to a blood-horse", said a breeder to me in Dublin, "they will breed nice show ponies", pointing to examples of miniature show-hacks that had won all before them at big shows in England, despite their nervous temperament and lack of bone. In Germany and Holland the demand is more for sturdy, pure-bred lines, whose great jumping potential under adolescent and adult riders, both at shows and in three-day events, as well as their ability in the dressage arena, commend them as the multi-purpose family horse.

Acclimatization. Connemara pony galloping in the snow of Upper Bavaria.

(*Kuhlmann, Munich*)

A successful team of Connemaras at a hunter trial in the United States. (*American Connemara Pony Society, Rochester*)

The charm of youth. A dressage team in Sweden, uniformly mounted on Connemara ponies. (*Heinz von Sterneck, Stockholm*)

The headquarters of the English Connemara Pony Society. Mrs Barthorp's stallion Sprig of Heather, the mare Grania, and two of their female offspring.

(Mrs. L. Barthorp, Farnham)

The gelding Irish Don (46) by Dun Lorenzo (55) out of Irish Peach (1366) has emigrated to Germany, losing nothing of his vigour and high spirits.

(*Richard Wagner, Munich*)

On the Isle of Lambay the brood mares are changing pasture . . .

. . . while far off on his hill the stallion tosses his head.

What of the Irish themselves? What do they want from the Connemara? An experienced horsewoman, a breeder and judge of ponies, who is also the mother of the highly successful Susan Lanigan O'Keefe, was quite definite about this. "So far as conformation goes, a small horse rather than a pony—only much closer to the ground. It is untypical of Connemaras to be high on the leg, and quite unpractical. Horses that live out all the year round should have short legs rather than long ones. The second thigh should come right down, and the hocks be broad and well under the pony. The action ought not to be too flat. Mountain ponies need to lift their feet up so as not to stumble on the rocky going. A rather long back is part of the picture; after all, this was once a pack pony on which the rider sat behind the load. The ribs should be well sprung, especially the mares should be roomy. Many Connemaras have deep-set eyes, which is a useful protection for grazing amongst thorns and sharp rocks, holly and thistles and briars."

There is in Ireland less objection in principle to cross-breeding than on the Continent, where the greatest objection is that 'blood' ponies have not the hardiness necessary for wintering out on hay, with perhaps an open box. But this consideration does not apply in Ireland, even though not all parts of it are as mild as Galway. Nevertheless, the Gulf Stream exerts its influence right through the island, where even Thoroughbreds are able to winter out. There are few east winds, and the grass stays green for a long time. Moreover, the Irish are better able to give a pony the kind of treatment its breeding requires—their knowledge of horses is deeper and more comprehensive than that of Continental peoples (with some exceptions).

Much more important than all this is the Irish passion for hunting, with their many packs of fox-hounds, harriers, and (carted) staghounds. The hunting season lasts from early October till April—a good half of the year. There are still a lot of people in Ireland who have time, or make time, to hunt two and three days a week throughout the season —and they are not all lords and ladies or retired admirals. They are farmers and young girls, old ladies and bank clerks, grocers and publicans and doctors and priests; a cross-section of the population. The wall-chequered pastures of the West, especially in Galway and Mayo and Sligo, become in the hunting season gigantic arenas of stone hedges and stone-faced banks. You just *have* to jump. In England there is always a gate in one corner of the field if you do not like the look of the fences. Not here. Once you are inside the maze of stone walls, there is no way out save over the top. In the West you jump or stay at home.

A Master of Harriers said to me gaily, "There's always something doing with us. If you went out without taking two hundred jumps I'd say you had a wasted afternoon."

A lady who up to the time of her marriage had hunted in England confessed to me that hunting in Galway put her in fear for her daughter's life, until the thirteen-year-old laughed her out of countenance. "The ponies know the way over—all you have to do is sit on top, and stay there. . . ."

Ponies of $13\frac{1}{2}$ or 14 hands, out after hounds, have to twist and turn, between high narrow walls, take standing jumps on to banks, perhaps with a thicket of brambles on the far side, or a heap of boulders, or a pool of bog water; what steely sinews, what sound feet, what courageous hearts they must have!

"Foreigners often ask me if it is not cruel to ask such relatively small animals to jump obstacles of this sort under a grown man. But there is no question of compulsion. One cannot *compel* a horse over a hundred fences in a row! And what would be the fun of riding, even for half an hour, a horse that had to be forced over fences? On the contrary, it often happens that a horse has been left out at grass and the hounds come that way. At the sound of the horn it will clear several high walls to get to the pack, and stay with them across country for hours at a time! These ponies learn to jump while they are foals at foot—how else could they follow their dams over the rough grazing?"

You had only to look round to see what the master meant. They were no tracks in the extra-Hibernian sense, and not a level rood of pasture or firm ground; either it is stony or it is boggy underfoot, and the horses have to be clever and at home on the rough ground, with a natural bent for going across this sort of country—which they have.

Some breeders are trying to exploit this natural aptitude for jumping, putting Connemara mares to Thoroughbred stallions, such as Little Heaven, whose progeny out of Connemara mares made headlines in the sporting Press. For instance, Smoky Joe and Dundrum—little horses with big hearts—won innumerable international competitions and national championships, beating horses that stood two hands taller than themselves. Little Model gained international fame as a dressage horse. He was third in the European championship of 1963, having carried Brenda Williams in the Rome Olympics of 1960. Korbous, out of a Connemara mare by a Barb stallion, was so successful that he appeared at the Horse of the Year Show at Wembley by invitation; he was ridden publicly by Penelope Morton, over obstacles and in the dressage arena without a bridle or reins to demonstrate his intelligence and good nature. [This has been a Barb speciality since antiquity. Classical writers speak of the Numidians fighting on horseback with only a neck-strap to guide the horse. These accounts were regarded as fables until modern times, when an enterprising officer of Spahis, serving with Commandant G. Lefebvre des Noëttes (who wrote the most penetrating history of the ridden horse ever to be composed in any language) put the veracity of the ancients to the test by training a Barb horse to go through all the motions of the Moroccan *Fantasia* using only a strap round the neck. *Tr.*].

The urge to inflate and accelerate the little 'jumping wonder' of Connemara by a cross of blood is understandable. But we should all deplore—in as much as we admire the tough, hardy type that lives wild among the Twelve Bens—any attempt to modify the breed itself in the pretty-pretty direction, making it more delicate if more successful in the show-ring, with really sensational victories from time to time. There are enough breeds of big, fast horses in the world. But the precious legacy of blood selected by nature itself ought not to be thrown away. Even among those who are in favour of out-crossing, there are some who counsel recourse to the lighter types of Irish Hunter

35

which have also been subjected to some extent to the natural selection of the Irish climate and environment, and have proved their worth in the Irish hunting field. [The practical difficulty about this is that among Irish hunters lighter types are in the minority, and any introduction of hunter blood would have to be 'indirect' and slow, since the Irish Hunter *stallion* hardly exists. Presumably the procedure would be to cover selected Connemara mares with a stallion by a Connemara sire out of an Irish Hunter mare. But this colt, once grown, would have to have time to demonstrate his own ability as a working hunter before being put to the pony mares. *Tr.*] It would be a pity, after all the centuries of the battle against nature, after all the effort that has been put into reversing the trend derived from mistaken breeding policy in the past, to sacrifice those qualities which so endear us to the 'genuine' pony in those countries where it exists: their honest, reliable temperament, their steady nerves, their sound constitution and superb bone, muscle, and sinew, their endurance under the saddle and ability to winter out—in short, all those qualities which they have inherited from primeval times, and which have suddenly put them at a premium in an age when there is a shortage of leisure (and of grooms) in most European countries to keep horses up and 'hard' fed in the traditional manner.

Outside Connemara

The breeding of these ponies has in the past decades re-expanded from Connemara to other parts of Ireland. I made excursions north and south to visit individual studs. At Abbeyleix, in the centre of the Irish Republic, we found a small stud in a delightful situation, with valuable stock amid old-established woodland. (Ireland is not, overall, a treeless country.) There are mature woodlands not lashed by the Atlantic winds where mixed stands of timber grow tall out of luxuriant undergrowth. Here ancient oaks alternated with rusty-boled pines to form coppices that were linked together in a parkland reminiscent of England. In the shade of these we found Connemara mares

Groups split off from the herd, look all around them . . .

. . . but soon settle down to the traditional game of mane-nibbling . . .

. . . grace-
fully
bending
their
slender
necks,
while their
dark eyes
look at us.

Late in the afternoon they are turned out again to the freedom of the hills . . .

. . . they march leisurely onward, in strict order of precedence . . .

. . . away from the paddocks with their scent of man . . .

. . . up to the windy knolls and the treeless valleys . . .

. . . where the only company is that of thousands of seagulls.

grazing with their foals. They have long since adapted themselves to their changed surroundings, and they gather in the shade of a mighty tree, their grey coats dappled with a shadow-pattern of leaves such as is unknown in the country of their birth.

Another breeder invited us to visit his stud on an island in the Irish Sea off the east coast, an hour's journey from Dublin. His private ferry put us ashore on Lambay—whose name is a legacy of the stock-breeding activity of the Ostmen Vikings; in Norse it means "the Isle of Lambs"—so that our last visit to the Connemara ponies reflected the same amalgam of wind and sea horses with which we had begun on the east coast.

The island is some 700 or 800 acres in extent. In a patch of woodland close to the shore stands an old, rose-grown castle of grey stone, centuries old. The owner, Lord Revelstoke, is a banker in London, but likes to spend as much time as he can in this sea-girt retreat, coming over as often as the heavy seas permit his ferry-boat to land. There are seventy ponies on the island, with the gulls tumbling in the windy sky above. They breed on the island, and besides these gulls it is full of birds (being, indeed, a bird sanctuary). Their varied cries fill the clear and salty air.

[The keeping of breeding-stock, and indeed fattening stock, of all kinds on small islands is characteristic of the whole North Atlantic–Irish Sea region, from Faeroe to Pembrokeshire. To the pastoralist of primitive times it offered the solution to many intractable problems at once, provided he had a boat with a solid enough bottom to transport full-grown cattle and horses. In the first place, it was relatively easy to eliminate wolves from a small isle; and they constituted Public Enemy Number One to the early stockbreeder; whereas on the mainland he might exterminate them on his own grazing-ground, and they creep back from the surrounding wilderness. In the second place, the need for fences did not exist—a major consideration in all ages until the invention of the wire fence. In the third place, selective breeding became possible at one stroke. A good stallion marooned with a band of mares has a better—and utterly exclusive—chance of getting them all in foal than the same stallion with the same mares on some mainland moor. In the fourth place, such islands are often much more free of snowfall than the mainland, even if they lie only a few miles off-shore, and much more fertile because of the seabirds mentioned above, who generation after generation enrich the soil with ample deposits of guano. That this form of stock husbandry has been practised by all the successive inhabitants of the region, regardless of race and language, is evident in the names of islands like Hestur ('stallion') in Faeroe; Horse Island in the Minch; numerous English Horse Islands, or Horseys; Inishbofin (White Bull Island), one off Donegal and one off Galway; Mutton Island off Clare, and several islets called Inish-na-Capall ('Isle of the Horse'), both in the Hebrides and off the Irish coast. *Tr.*]

They brought the ponies down for us to gently sloping in-field, so that we could study them at leisure. A world of maternity and curiosity enfolded us. We are hemmed in by muzzles and legs and bent heads and sniffing nostrils. Slowly the ponies graze towards us—towards the very spot where I am sitting, making notes. The wind ruffles up their manes, a soft nose brushes my face, delicate whiskers tickle my cheek like a fly crawling over it, and a warm breath blows over me. One more step and I am sitting between four legs, under a broad belly. They are legs like pillars, and rather frightening, though the pony is so quiet. Mares are always jealous towards each other, and a kick that merely lends emphasis as between horses can be quite damaging to the human frame.

Moreover, six dozen honest, inquisitive, importunate horses of various ages and varying intelligence are a barely insurable risk to such items as cameras, note-books, tape recorders, and spare films, so that I soon take refuge on the far side of the hedge, leaving my photographer flat on his belly among them, trying to record pictorially the curve of a neck and their innocent unconscious grace, the intensity of their nibbling at each other's rough manes.

All about us the sea stretches grey-green and light blue under a light breeze. Most of the horses are grey, with here and there a bay or black, and the grey comes in all shades. There are a few beautiful duns, with thick black manes matted by the salt wind. The gulls scream above us, while from the stables below comes the call of a stallion.

The bond between such ponies and their native landscape is so much closer than in the case of horses which are kept up. This is so all over the world. Even when they are transplanted to another landscape, the scent of summer grasses and the mouldering smell of ponds hangs about them. They are wrapped in the freshness of the sea-wind, the chill of the snowstorm. All their lives long they—and their forefathers—have used their ears to sift the significant sounds out of the manifold symphony of freedom, and their eyes to search the surface of the land, ever on the watch; knowing every stick and stone and blade of sea-ware, knowing every stream in drought and in flood, the foreshore at every stage of the tide. They know the roaring breakers and the soft lapping of wavelets on the summer strand. They have plodded through the reeds and the rushes and stepped out over the rocks, forcing their way through bush and briar; galloped up the slopes; and thus their senses are more amply filled than those of stabled horses, their horizon is wider and their memory more stored with images than the 'indoor' horse that knows only one climate, one kind of food, one man-made abiding-place. They remember the wind singing in their manes, the cool earth of summer nights, and the encircling warmth of their thick winter coats.

But these Connemaras have grown up on an island, in tranquillity and seclusion. There is a whispering and a rustling constantly about them; wading birds nest in the marsh reeds, mice and partridges brush past at their feet, the crying of gulls is in their ears at the moment of birth.

And we take them away from here to a far country, perhaps to another continent, and give them what we value ourselves—warmth and cleanliness, security and abundant food. But do we not often starve their senses? Do we give them enough of what they really need—close proximity to the whole of nature, at all times and seasons? Are we doing to them what we have done to our 'civilized' horses for so long, until inevitably and irreversibly they have become duller and more indifferent? Do we lodge them in a narrow, airless stable, setting always the same food before them, not scrupling even to cross them with other breeds, thus robbing them of their full and complete individuality? Such thoughts went through my mind as I sat in the midst of that rich, insistent natural scene.

We had been to Connemara and seen its ponies in their splendid freedom, watched them, listened to them, listened about them, photographed them. Now we followed them to Lambay Island, and watched the herd being turned out on the hill, sedately filing in strict order of precedence, without haste, in the security of their established social life, free internally as externally.

The sky darkened to westward, the wind swept the gulls up into the sky. The horses calmly awaited the storm which they knew was brewing.

"Out of endless space a wind swept down through the empty chambers of the night" sang a Connemara bard of such a moment; "It struck the earth with the sound of thunder, and tore the fleece of the heavens apart." And through it all sounded the singing voices of the fairy folk:

> . . . the gales are hounds,
> And they hunt together with our horses.
> See now our horses. Their manes are clouds.
> The ground gapes in chasms below their feet
> As we ride, cleaving the air;
> But the horses are not dismayed . . .